My Best Buddy M.L.

By G.L. Marini
Inspired by M.L. Marini

Illustrations by Tom Arvis

Dedication:

This book is dedicated to my best friend and gorgeous wife, M.L. We were really young when we met and became, over time, thanks to my dogged determination, the best of friends. We believe in and are always there for each other.

When I told M.L. I was going to write children's books, she was supportive and encouraging. Somehow, she believes in me more than I believe in myself. I adore my M.L. and am so grateful to share every day of life with her. Thank you so much for your love and devotion my M.L. This book is for you!

So, my name is Guy and when I was about 8 years old...
I loved peanut butter and cheese burgers but my favorite was
pizza. Boy, do I love pizza.

My best friends were Bobby, Ralphy, Freddie, Pompy and
Ido. We played ball, hide and seek, tag and just about every
me you could imagine.

I had really nice neighbors...there was a Mom and Dad and this little girl named M. L., short for Mary Lee.

I really didn't like girls. They seemed to like to sit around, play dolls and drink tea, well...make believe tea...

I didn't like tea. My Mom used to make tea, let it cool and put it on my skin when I had a sunburn.

So why would anyone ever drink tea or drink it make believe? Doesn't make any sense.

One day M.L. brought some sidewalk chalk over. I told her I couldn't really draw. She said, "Oh, I can draw really good – want to see?"

Well, I was amazed! M. L., with her strawberry blond hair and blue eyes and freckles, got on her hands and knees and drew the most beautiful drawing I had ever seen.

It was a big house with huge oak trees on each side. There were 2 kids playing catch in the yard and a beautiful dog was running. I told her she was the best artist in the world!

Let me tell you, she gave me the biggest and prettiest smile I had ever seen and said, "Thank you – I love to draw! Do you want me to teach you?"

Well, I tried and M. L. said I was doing really good. I drew a football field with players on it.

My Dad came home and said, "Hi M. L....Hi Guy...Hey Guy, that is a really nice picture of a bunch of guys sitting on their rear ends." My Dad really isn't the greatest artist either or he has bad eye sight.

About a week later, I got a brand new pair of black rollerblades with flames painted on them for my birthday. They were really cool. I couldn't wait to get them on.

I went out on the sidewalk and couldn't make it 3 feet without falling down. Finally, I went about 10 feet and fell into my neighbor's barrels knocking them all over with milk bottles, newspapers and trash bags on the ground, and all over me.

M.L. and her father came running out and asked if I was hurt. Well I was but I didn't admit it.

M.L.'s Dad said, "M.L., you are a pretty good rollerblader—why don't you show Guy how to rollerblade without destroying our trash?"

She smiled that big smile of hers where her cheeks looked like rosy red apples and said "OK!".

Well, wouldn't you know! M. L. could rollerblade like crazy. She had great balance and was able to teach me.

Well, from that day on I asked her Mom and Dad if she could rollerblade with me and she always said yes.

She wasn't really a best friend or anything. I still didn't like girls but M. L. was pretty good at drawing and rollerblading.

Sometimes M.L.'s parents and my Mom and Dad would have a cook out.

They were very, very fun – no pizza - usually cheeseburgers and hot dogs and lemonade and ice cream.

I was having a really nice summer and one day a lot
f our friends and neighbors decided we would all go to the
each.

Ne had a blast! My best buds and I played football in the
and.

The girls were hunting for sea shells and our parents made us nice food and had cold drinks for us- we were living it up!

Well, people started to leave but we were staying and so was M. L.'s family.

I asked her if she wanted to do anything with me. She asked if we could build a sand fort together with our pails and shovels. I jumped at the chance.

So I was the worker/builder and she was the architect.

She had this idea that we could build sand walls with tower and dig a moat all around the sand fort.

Well, we worked hard together and were a good team.

Pretty soon people would walk by and say things like "That is a great sand fort! How long have you two been working on this? It's fantastic."

M. L. and I were beaming with pride.

Well, we wrapped up the day and took pictures of
ourselves – just M. L. and me in front of our world class san
fort.

We shook hands and M. L. said, "We are a great team, Guy!
I think we can do anything." And I said, "You know M. L.,
you're right we are a great team."

The next thing I knew we were walking off the beach carrying our stuff.

M. L. and I were talking and laughing and I realized that I could have a girl who could be a best friend.

I couldn't believe that I was thinking that but I was.

I felt pretty good and said to M. L., "Hey M. L., we probably should get married. What do you think?"

She told me she was 8 and no one had asked her to get married but said, "Let me think about it."

When I went to bed that night I realized that for a boy to get married you are suppose to give the girl a ring.

My Mom has a nice ring. Actually, she has a lot of rings so I borrowed one.

The next morning I saw M. L. and asked if she thought about my idea to get married.

She said she was still thinking about it. I showed her the ring that I borrowed from my Mom.

She really, really liked it...so I said, "While you are thinking about my marriage proposal, M. L., go ahead and wear it."

Shortly after that I learned that you really couldn't get married at 8 and 9 years old even if you really liked someone like M.L.

Something about being older, growing up, getting a degree or a skill of some kind...stuff like that. M.L. and I both went along with our parent's advice; but, we did decide to be best friends.

Oh yeah, M. L. gave my Mom's ring back to me and I gave it back to my Mom.

My Mom was sort of laughing and shaking her head. I guess that wasn't such a great idea after all... but it did seem to be the right thing to do at the time. Next time, I'll ask my Mom if it's OK.

Guess what, about 50 years later, we still like each other and we are still best friends.

The only trouble is she always reminds me she taught me how to draw, rollerblade and led the building of a really nice sand fort.

You'd think after being best friends for 50 years she could let it go!

So...if you are a girl, do you think it's OK to have a boy as a good or best friend?

Or if you are a boy, do you think it's OK to have a girl as a good or best friend? What do you think?

Draw a picture about the story!

Draw a picture of M.L. and Guy!

Other **Super Nonno** Books by Guy Marini Available on Amazon.com :
Super Nonno - The Adventures of Super Nonno
For The Love of Freckles
Little Miss Excitement
For The Love of Pizza
The Boy Who Loved Trucks
Patsy, Pipi & Duke

Made in the USA
Middletown, DE
19 September 2021